SWE

SWAHILI

A Fantastic Phrasebook for Beginners

MOTHERLAND LITERATURE

"Sweet Swahili – A Fantastic Phrasebook for Beginners"

Motherland Literature© 2021

(motherlandliterature@gmail.com)

@motherlandliterature

Cover photograph:
©istockphoto.com/portifolio/tempura

MOTHERLAND

LITERATURE

CONTENTS

SPECIAL BONUS

Want this bonus book for <u>free?</u>

Get <u>FREE</u> unlimited access to this and all our new books by joining our community!

SCAN w/ your camera TO JOIN!

About Swahili

Swahili, or Kiswahili, belongs to the Benue-Congo branch of the Niger-Congo language family. Swahili is spoken in East Africa by different countries along the coast from Somalia to Mozambique.

The use of Swahili spread with the growth of commerce during the colonial period in the 19th-20th centuries.

Alongside English, Swahili is the official language of Tanzania, Kenya, and Uganda, and is the only African language of the African Union. Swahili is also spoken in Malawi, Burundi, Mozambique, Rwanda, Somalia, Democratic Republic of Congo, Zambia and Uganda.

Swahili is fast becoming increasingly important in politics, commerce, culture, education, and mass media.

Significantly, Swahili is the only African language among the official working languages of the African Union.

Numbers

Namba *(nah-m-bah)*

0. Zero – Sifuri
(see-foo-ree)

1. One – Moja
(moo-jah)

2. Two – Mbili
(mbee-lee)

3. Three – Tatu
(tah-too)

4. Four – Nne
(n-neh)

5. Five – Tano
(tah –noo)

6. Six – Sita
(see-tah)

7. Seven – Saba
(sah-bah)

8. Eight – Nane
(nah-neh)

9. Nine – Tisa
(tee-sah)

10. Ten – Kumi
(koo-meh)

11. Eleven - Kumi na Moja
(koo-meh-nah-moh-jah)

12. Twelve – Kumi na Mbili
(koo-meh-nah-mbee-lee)

13. Thirteen – Kumi na Tanu
(koo-meh-nah-tah-too)

14. Fourteen – Kumi na Nne
(koo-meh-nah-n-neh)

15. Fifteen - Kumi na Tano
(koo-meh-nah-tah-noh)

16. Sixteen - Kumi na Sita
(koo-meh-nah-see-tah)

17. Seventeen - Kumi na Saba
(koo-meh-nah-sah-bah)

18. Eighteen - Kumi na Nane
(koo-meh-nah-nah-neh)

19. Nineteen - Kumi na Tisa
(koo-meh-nah-tee-sah)

20. Twenty – Ishirini
(ee-shee-ree-nee)

21. Twenty-one – Ishirini na Moja
(ee-shee-ree-nee-nah-moh-jah)

22. Twenty-two - Ishirini na Mbili
(ee-shee-ree-nee-nah-mbee-lee)

23. Twenty-three - Ishirini na Tatu
(ee-shee-ree-nee-nah-tah-too)

24. Twenty-four - Ishirini na Nne
(ee-shee-ree-nee-nah-n-neh)

25. Twenty-five - Ishirini na Tano
(ee-shee-ree-nee-nah-tah-noh)

26. Twenty-six - Ishirini na Sita
(ee-shee-ree-nee-nah-see-tah)

27. Twenty-seven - Ishirini na Saba
(ee-shee-ree-nee-nah-sah-bah)

28. Twenty-eight - Ishirini na Nane
(ee-shee-ree-nee-nah-nah-neh)

29. Twenty-nine - Ishirini na Tisa
(ee-shee-ree-nee-nah-tee-sah)

30. Thirty – Thelathini
(theh-lah-thee-nee)

31. Thirty-one – Thelathini na Moja
(theh-lah-thee-nee-nah-moh-jah)

32. Thirty-two - Thelathini na mbili
(theh-lah-thee-nee-nah-mbee-lee)

33. Thirty-three - Thelathini na tatu
(theh-lah-thee-nee-nah-tah-too)

40. Forty – Arobaini
(Ah-roh-bah-ee-nee)

50. Fifty – Hamsini
(Hah-m-see-nee)

60. Sixty – Sitini
(See-tee-nee)

70. Seventy – Sabini
(sah-bee-nee)

80. Eighty – Themanini
(theh-mah-nee-nee)

90. Ninety – Tisini
(tee-see-nee)

100. One hundred – Mia moja
(mee-ah-moh-jah)

101. One hundred and one - Mia moja na moja
(mee-ah-moh-jah-nah-moh-jah)

102. One hundred and two - Mia moja na mbili
(mee-ah-moh-jah-nah-mbee-lee)

154. One hundred and fifty-four - Mia moja
hamsini na nne
(mee-ah-moh-jah-hah-m-see-nee-nah-n-neh)

1000. One thousand – Elfu moja
(eh-l-foo-moh-jah)

1000000 - One million – Milioni moja
(mee-lee-oh-nee-moh-jah)

THE MONTHS
Miezi *(mee-eh-zee)*

January – Januari
(jah-noo-ah-ree)

February – Februari
(feh-broo-ah-ree)

March – Machi
(mah-chee)

April – Aprili
(ah-pree-lee)

May – Mei
(meh-ee)

June – Juni
(joo-nee)

July – Julai
(joo-lah-ee)

August – Agosti

(ah-goh-stee)

September – Septemba
(seh-p-teh-mbah)

October – Oktoba
(oh-k-toh-bah)

November – Novemba
(noh-veh-mbah)

December – Disemba
(dee-seh-mbah)

THE DAYS OF THE WEEK

(and related phrases) – Siku za wiki (na misemo inayoendana) *(see-koo-zah-wee-kee (nah-mee-seh-moh-ee-nah-yoh-eh-ndah-nah)*

Monday – Juma tatu
(joo-mah-tah-too)

Tuesday – Juma nne
(joo-mah-n-neh)

Wednesday – Juma tano
(joo-mah-tah-noh)

Thursday – Alhamisi
(ah-l-hah-mee-see)

Friday – Ijumaa
(ee-joo-mah-ah)

Saturday – Juma mosi
(joo-mah-moh-see)

Sunday – Juma pili
(joo-mah-pee-lee)

Today – Leo
(leh-oh)

This morning – Asubuhi hii
(ah-soo-boo-hee-hee-hee)

In the afternoon – Mchana
(m-chah-nah)

In the evening - Jioni
(jee-oh-nee)

At night – Usiku
(oo-see-koo)

Tomorrow – Kesho
(keh-shoh)

Yesterday – Jana
(jah-nah)

Last night – Jana usiku
 (jah-nah-oo-see-koo)

Where were you last night? – Ulikuwa wapi usiku wa jana?
(oo-lee-koo-wah-wah-pee-oo-see-koo-wah-jah-nah-?)

What day is it today? – Leo ni siku gani?
(leh-oh-nee-see-koo-gah-nee-?)

THE PEOPLE

Family members/People – Ndugu wa familia/Watu *(ndoo-goo-wah-fah-mee-lee-ah/wah-too)*

Mother – Mama
(mah-mah)

Father – Baba
(bah-bah)

Brother – Kaka
(kah-kah)

Sister – Dada
(dah-dah)

Daughter – Binti
(bee-n-tee)

Son – Kijana
(kee-jah-nah)

Woman - Mwanamke
(mwah-nah-m-keh)

Girl – **Msichana**
(m-see-chah-nah)

Man- **Mwanaume**
(mwah-nah-oo-meh)

Boy – **Mvulana**
(m-voo-lah-nah)

Child – **Mtoto**
(m-toh-toh)

Twin – **Mapacha**
(mah-pah-chah)

Children – Mtoto
(m-toh-toh)

Parent – Mzazi
(m-zah-zee)

Parents – Wazazi
(wah-zah-zee)

Brother – Kaka
(kah-kah)

Sister – Dada
(dah-dah)

Older sibling – Ndugu mkubwa
(ndoo-goo-m-koo-bwah)

Younger sibling – Ndugu mdogo
(ndoo-goo-m-doh-goh)

Uncle – Mjomba
(m-joh-mbah)

Auntie – Shangazi
(shah-ngah-zee)

Wife – Mke
(m-keh)

Husband - Mume
(moo-meh)

Father of children – Baba wa mtoto
(bah-bah-wah-m-toh-toh)

Mother of children – Mama wa mtoto
(mah-mah-wah-m-toh-toh)

Brother in law – Shemeji
(sheh-meh-jee)

Sister in law – Wifi / shemeji
(wee-fee/sheh-meh-jee)

Grandmother – Bibi
(bee-bee)

Grandfather – Babu
(bah-boo)

Old – Mzee
(m-zeh-eh)

Young – Kijana
(kee-jah-nah)

People – Watu
(wah-too)

Friend – Rafiki
(rah-fee-kee)

PARTS OF THE BODY

Sehemu za mwili
(seh-heh-moo-zah-mwee-lee)

Human body – Mwili wa binadamu
(mwee-lee-wah-bee-nah-dah-moo)

Bone – Mfupa
(m-foo-pah)

Brain – Ubongo
(oo-boh-ngoh)

Head – Kichwa
(kee-ch-wah)

Forehead – Paji la uso
(pah-jee-lah-oo-soh)

Face – Sura
(soo-rah)

Cheek – Shavu
(shah-voo)

Ear – Sikio
(see-kee-oh)

Ears - Masikio
(mah-see-kee-oh)

Eye – Jicho
(jee-choh)

Ears - Macho
(mah-choh)

Nose – Pua
(poo-ah)

Mouth – Mdomo
(m-doh-moh)

Chin – Kidevu
(kee-deh-voo)

Throat – Koo
(koh-oh)

Lips – Midomo
(mee-doh-moh)

Tongue – Ulimi
(oo-lee-mee)

Tooth – Jino
(jee-noh)

Teeth – Meno
(meh-noh)

Neck – Shingo
(shee-ngoh)

Arm – Mkono
(m-koh-noh)

Arms - Mikono
(mee-koh-noh)

Armpits – Kwapa
(kwah-pah)

Hand – Mkono
(m-koh-noh)

Hands - Mikono
(mee-koh-noh)

Finger – Kidole
(kee-doh-leh)

Fingers – Vidole
(vee-doh-leh)

Nail – Kucha
(koo-chah)

Chest – Kifua
(kee-foo-ah)

Back – Mgongo
(m-goh-ngoh)

Stomach – Tumbo
(too-mboh)

Belly button – Kitovu
(kee-toh-voo)

Breast – Ziwa
(zee-wah)

Breasts - Maziwa
(mah-zee-wah)

Penis – Uume
(oo-meh)

Vagina – Uke
(oo-keh)

Buttocks – Matako
(mah-tah-koh)

Anus – Mkundu
(m-koo-ndoo)

Hip – Nyonga
(nyoh-ngah)
Thigh – Paja
(pah-jah)

Knee – Goti
(goh-tee)

Leg– Mguu
(m-goo)

Legs - Miguu
(mee-goo)

Foot – Mguu
(m-goo)

Feet - Miguu
(mee-goo)

Toe – Kidole
(kee-doh-leh)

Skin – Ngozi
(ngoh-zee)

Heart – Moyo
(moh-yoh)

Muscle – Msuli
(m-soo-lee)

Blood – Damu
(dah-moo)

Hair – Nywele
(ny-weh-leh)

Beard – Ndevu
(ndeh-voo)

PRONOUNS
Viwakilishi *(vee-wah-kee-lee-shee)*

I – Mimi
(mee-mee)

Me – Mimi
(mee-mee)

My – Wangu
(wah-ngoo)

Mine - Yangu
(yah-ngoo)

You – Wewe
(weh-weh)

He – Yeye (Mvulana)
(yeh-yeh) (m-voo-lah-nah)

She – Yeye (Msichana)
(yeh-yeh) (m-see-chah-nah)

Hers – Yake (Msichana)
(yah-keh) (m-see-chah-nah)

His –Yake (Mvulana)
(yah-keh) (m-voo-lah)

We – Sisi
(see-see)

They are – Wao ni
(wah-oh-nee)

Them – **Wao**
(wah-oh)

Us – **Sisi**
(see-see)

Yours – **Yako**
(yah-koh)

It – **Ni**
(nee)

Myself – Mimi mwenyewe
(mee-mee-mweh-nyeh-weh)

Yourself – *Wewe mwenyewe*
(weh-weh-mweh-nyeh-weh)

Himself - Yeye mwenyewe (mwanaume)
(yeh-yeh-mweh-nyeh-weh) (mwah-nah-oo-meh)

Herself – Yeye mwenyewe (mwanamke)
(yeh-yeh- mweh-nyeh-weh) (mwah-nah-m-keh)

Itself – Yenyewe
(yeh-nyeh-weh)

Ourselves – Sisi wenyewe
(see-see-weh-nyeh-weh)

Themselves – Wao wenyewe
(wah-oh-weh-nyeh-weh)

Yourselves – Nyinyi wenyewe
(nyee-nyee-weh-nyeh-weh)

This – Hii
(hee-ee)

That – Kile
(kee-leh)

ADVERBS
Vielezi *(vee-eh-leh-zee)*

Here – Hapa
(hah-pah)

There – Pale
(pah-leh)

Up – Juu
(joo)

Down – Chini
(chee-nee)

Near – Karibu
(kee-ree-boo)

Close - Karibia
(Kah-ree-bee-ah)

Far/Away – Mbali
(mbah-lee)

VERBS
Vitenzi *(vee-teh-zee)*

To be – Kuwa
(koo-wah)

To begin/start – Kuanza/anza
(koo-ah-nzah/ah-nzah)

To stop – Kusimama
(koo-see-mah-mah)

To end – Kumaliza
(koo-mah-lee-zah)

To find – Kutafuta
(koo-tah-foo-tah)

To lose – Kupoteza
(koo-poh-teh-zah)

To think – Kufikiria
(koo-fee-kee-ree-ah)

To give – Kutoa
(koo-toh-ah)

To take – Kuchukua
(koo-choo-koo-ah)

To steal – Kuiba
(koo–ee-bah)

To hide – Kuficha
(koo-fee-chah)

To keep – Kubakinacho
(koo-bah-kee-nah-choh)

To come – Kuja
(koo-jah)

To leave – Kuondoka
(koo-oh-ndoh-kah)

To go – Kwenda
(kweh-ndah)

To go back – Kurudi
(koo-roo-dee)

To meet – Kukutana
(koo-too-kah-nah)

To say – Kusema
(koo-seh-mah)

To speak – Kuongea
(koo-oh-ngeh-ah)

To pray – Kusali/Kuswali
(koo-sah-lee/koo-swah-lee)

To preach – Kuhubiri
(koo-hoo-bee-ree)

To see – Kuona
(koo-oh-nah)

To look – **Kuangalia**
(koo-ah-ngah-lee-ah)

To hear – Kusikia
(koo-see-kee-ah)

To touch – Kugusa
(koo-goo-sah)

To come – Kuja
(koo-jah)

To come from – Kuja kutoka
(koo-jah-koo-toh-kah)

To come back – Kurudi
(koo-roo-dee)

To sell – Kuuza
(koo-oo-zah)

To buy – Kununua
(koo-noo-noo-ah)

To insult – Kutukana
(koo-toh-kah-nah)

To be sick – Kuwa mgonjwa
(koo-wah-m-goh-jwah)

To get better – Kuwa vizuri
(koo-wah-vee-zoo-ree)

To worry – Kuwa na wasiwasi
(koo-wah-nah-wah-see-wah-see)

To boil – Kuchemsha
(koo-cheh-m-shah)

To fry – Kukausha
(koo-kah-oo-shah)

To cook – Kupika
(koo-pee-kah)

To eat – Kula
(koo-lah)

To drink – Kunywa
(koo-ny-wah)

To vomit – Kutapika
(koo-tah-pee-kah)

To believe - Kuamini
(koo-ah-mee-nee)

To accept - Kukubali
(koo-koo-bah-lee)

To refuse/reject- Kukataa
(koo-kah-tah-ah)

To deny – Kukataa
(koo-kah-tah-ah)

To send – Kutuma
(koo-too-mah)

To leave – Kuondoka
(koo-oh-ndoh-kah)

To arrive – Kufika
(koo-fee-kah)

To hold – Kusimamisha
(koo-see-mah-mee-shah)

To get – Kuchukua
(koo-choo-koo-ah)

To fix – Kutengeneza
(koo-teh-ngeh-neh-zah)

To make – Kutengeneza
(koo-teh-ngeh-neh-zah)

To build/construct – Kujenga
(koo-jeh-ngah)

To cut – Kukata
(koo-kah-tah)

To break - Kata
(kah-tah)

To smash – Kubamiza
(koo-bah-meh-zah)

To spread – Kutawanya
(koo-tah-wah-nyah)

To grow – Kukuwa
(koo-koo-wah)

To leave – Kuondoka
(koo-oh-ndoh-kah)

To add – Kuongeza
(koo-oh-ngeh-zah)

To remove – Kuondoa
(koo-oh-ndoh-kah)

To stick – Kugandisha
(koo-gah-ndee-shah)

To have – Kuwa nayo
(koo-wah-nah-yoh)

To lack – Kukosa
(koo-koh-sah)

To keep – Kuweka
(koo-weh-kah)

To throw away – Kutupa
(koo-too-pah)

To hang – Kunyonga
(koo-nyoh-ngah)

To stand – Kusimama
(koo-see-mah-mah)

To sit – Kukaa
(koo-kah-ah)

To do – Kufanya
(koo-fah-nyah)

To show – Kuonyesha
(koo-oh-nyeh-shah)

To choose – Kuchagua
(koo-chah-goo-ah)

To work – Kufanya kazi
(koo-fah-nyah-kah-zee)

To study – Kusoma
(koo-soh-mah)

To read – Kusoma
(koo-soh-mah)

To write – Kuandika
(koo-ah-ndee-kah)

To learn – Kujifunza
(koo-jee-foo-nzah)

To teach – Kufundisha
(koo-foo-ndee-shah)

To call – Kuita
(koo-ee-tah)

To shout – Kupiga kelele
(koo-pee-gah-keh-leh-leh)

To sing – Kusoma
(koo-soh-mah)

To dance – Kucheza
(koo-cheh-zah)

To talk – Kuongea
(koo-oh-ngeh-ah)

To laugh – Kucheka
(koo-cheh-kah)

To make laugh – Kuchekesha
(koo-cheh-keh-shah)

To be happy – Kuwa na furaha
(koo-wah-nah-foo-rah-hah)

To be sad – Kuwa na huzuni
(koo-wah-nah-hoo-zoo-nee)

To cry – Kulia
(koo-lee-ah)

To know – Kujua
(koo-joo-ah)

To deny – Kukataa
(koo-kah-tah-ah)

To fear – Kuogopa
(koo-oh-goh-pah)

To sleep – Kulala
(koo-lah-lah)

To wake up – Kuamka
(koo-ah-m-kah)

To become – Kuwa
(koo-wah)

To draw – Kuchora
(koo-choh-rah)

To follow – Kufuata
(koo-foo-ah-tah)

To like/love – Kupenda/penda
(koo-peh-ndah/peh-ndah)

To hug – Kukumbatia
(koo-koo-mbah-tee-ah)

To hate – Kuchukia
(koo-choo-kee-ah)

To give birth – Kuzaa
(koo-zah-ah)

To die – Kufa
(koo-fah)

To shake – Kutikisa
(koo-tee-kee-sah)

To be different – Kuwa tofauti
(koo-wah-toh-fah-oo-tee)

ADJECTIVES
Vivumishi *(vee-voo-mee-shee)*

Beautiful – Rembo
(reh-mboh)

Good – Nzuri
(nzoo-ree)

Bad/Ugly – Mbaya
(mbah-yah)

Big – Kubwa
(koo-bwah)

Fat – Nene
(neh-neh)

Small – **Ndogo**
(ndoh-goh)

Thin – **Nyembamba**
(nyeh-mbah-mbah)

-

Tall – Ndefu
(ndeh-foo)

Short – Fupi
(foo-pee)

Angry/Anger – Hasira
(hah-see-rah)

Happy – Furaha
(foo-rah-hah)

Sad – Uzuni
(oo-zoo-ree)

Embarrassed – Aibu
(ah-ee-boo)

Dark – Giza
(gee-zah)

Light – Mwanga
(mwah-ngah)

Hot – Joto
(joh-toh)

Cold – Baridi
(bah-ree-dee)

Old – Mzee
(m-zeh-eh)

Young – Kijana
(kee-jah-nah)

Crazy – Tahira
(tah-hee-rah)

Clever – Yenye akili
(yeh-nyeh-ah-kee-lee)

Stupid – Kichaa
(kee-chah-ah)

Lazy – Vivu
(vee-voo)

Slow – Pole pole
(poh-leh-poh-leh)

Fast – Haraka
(hah-rah-kah)

Noisy - Kelele
(keh-leh-leh)

Quiet – Kimya
(kee-m-yah)

Clean – Safi
(sah-fee)

Dirty - Chafu
(chah-foo)

Soft – Laini
(lah-ee-nee)

Hard – Ngumu
(ngoo-moo)

Thick – Nene
(neh-neh)

Sweet – Tamu
(tah-moo)

Salty – Yenye chumvi
(yeh-nyeh-choo-m-vee)

Sour – Chachu
(chah-choo)

Bitter – Chungu
(choo-ngoo)

Smooth – Laini
(lah-ee-nee)

Sunny – Yenye jua
(yeh-nyeh-joo-ah)

COLOURS

Rangi *(rah-ngee)*

Black – Nyeusi
(nyeh-oo-see)

White – Nyeupe
(nyeh-oo-peh)

Grey – Kijivu
(kee-jee-voo)

Blue – Bluu
(bloo-oo)

Green – Kijani
(kee-jah-nee)

Yellow – Njano
(njah-noh)

Brown – Kahawia
(kah-hah-wee-ah)

Orange – Rangi ya chungwa
(rah-ngee-yah-choo-ng-wah)

Red – Nyekundu
(nyeh-koo-ndoo)

Purple – Zambarau
(zah-mbah-rah-oo)

Foods – Vyakula
(vyah-koo-lah)

Bread and butter – Mkate na siagi
(m-kah-teh-wah-see-ah-gee)

Cassava bread – Mkate wa muogo
(m-kah-teh-wah-moo-oh-goh)

Eggs - Mayai
(mah-yah-ee)

Boiled egg – Yai la kuchemsha
(yah-ee-lah-koo-sheh-m-shah)

Fried eggs – Mayai ya kukaanga
(mah-yah-ee-yah-koo-kah-ah-ngah)

Raw egg – Yai bichi
(yah-ee-bee-chee)

Honey – Asali
(ah-sah-lee)

Avocado – Parachichi
(pah-rah-chee-chee)

Banana – Ndizi
(ndee-zee)

Plantain – Platani (ndizi za kukaanga)
(plah-tah-nee(ndee-zee-zah-koo-kah-ah-ngah)

Orange – Chungwa
(choo-ng-wah)

Lemon – **Limau**
(lee-mah-oo)

Coconut – **Nazi**
(nah-zee)

Papaya – **Papai**
(pah-pah-ee)

Guava – **Pera**
(peh-rah)

Grapefruit – **Zabibu**
(zah-bee-boo)

Mango – Embe
(eh-mbeh)

Ham – Nyama ya paja la nguruwe
(nyah-mah-yah-nyoo-roo-weh)

Salt - Chumvi
(choo-m-vee)

Sugar - Sukari
(soo-kah-ree)

Water – Maji
(mah-jee)

Milk - Maziwa
(mah-zee-wah)

Orange Juice – Juisi ya machungwa
(joo-ee-see-yah-mah-choo-ng-wah)

Tea - Chai
(chah-ee)

Coffee – Kahawa
(kah-hah-wah)

Beer – Bia
(bee-ah)

Animal – Mnyama
(m-nyah-mah)

Meat – Nyama
(nyah-mah)

Beef – Nyama ya n'gombe
(nyah-mah-yah-ng'oh-mbeh)

Goat – Mbuzi
(mboo-zee)

Chicken - Kuku
(koo-koo)

Mutton – Nyama ya kondoo
(nyah-mah-yah-koh-mdoh-oh)

Lamb - Kondoo
(koh-ndoh-oh)

Pork - Nguruwe
(ngoo-roo-weh)

Duck - Bata
(bah-tah)

Crab – Kaa
(kah-ah)

Eel – Eeli
(eh-eh-lee)

Fish – Samaki
(sah-mah-kee)

Salted fish – Samaki wa maji chumvi
(sah-mah-kee-wah-mah-jee-choo-m-vee)

Smoked fish – Samaki wa moshi
(sah-mah-kee-wah-moh-shee)

Sardines - Dagaa
(dah-gah-ah)

Shrimp – Uduvi/dagaa kamba
(oo-doo-vee/dah-gah-ah-kah-mbah)

Vegetable – Mboga mboga
(mboh-gah-mboh-gah)

Cassava leaf – Kisamvu
(kee-sah-m-voo)

Eggplant/Aubergine - Bilinganya
(bee-lee-ngah-nyah)

Onions – Vitunguu
(vee-too-ngoo-oo)

Garlic – Kitunguu swaumu
(kee-too-ngoo-oo-swah-oo-moo)

Yam - Tamu
(tah-moo)

Rice - Mchele
(m-cheh-leh)

Beans - Maharage
(mah-hah-rah-geh)

Tomatoes – Nyanya
(nyah-nyah)

Oil – Mafuta
(mah-foo-tah)

Pepper – Pilipili
(pee-lee-pee-lee)

ANIMALS
Wanyama *(wah-nyah-mah)*

Baboon - Ngedere
(ngeh-deh-reh)

Buffalo - Nyati
(nyah-tee)

Chimpanzee – Nyani
(nyah-nee)

Crocodile – Mamba
(mah-mbah)

Elephant – Tembo
(teh-mboh)

Giraffe – Twiga
(twee-gah)

Hyena – Fisi
(fee-see)

Hippopotamus – Kiboko
(kee-boh-goh)

Leopard – Chui
(choo-ee)

Lion - Simba
(see-mbah)

Monkey – Nyani
(nyah-nee)

Python - Chatu
(chah-too)

Wild Boar – Nguruwe pori
(ngoo-roo-weh-poh-ree)

Zebra – Pundamilia
(poo-ndah-mee-lee-ah)

HOUSEHOLD OBJECTS

Vitu vya *Nyumba (vee-too-vyah-nyoo-mbah-nee)*

Food – Chakula
(chah-koo-lah)

House – Nyumba
(nyoo-mbah)

Living room – Sebuleni
(seh-boo-leh-nee)

Bedroom – Chumbani
(choo-mbah-nee)

Bathroom – Bafuni
(bah-foo-nee)

Mirror – Kioo
(kee-oh-oh)

Garden - Bustani
(boo-stah-nee)

Land – Ardhi
(Ah-r-dhee)

Key – Funguo
(foo-ngoo-oh)

Table – Meza
(meh-zah)

Chair – Kiti
(kee-tee)

Bed – Kitanda
(kee-tah-ndah)

Plate – Sahani
(sah-hah-nee)

Spoon – Kijiko
(kee-jee-koh)

Folk – Uma
(oo-mah)

Knife – Kisu
(kee-soo)

Cup – Kikombe
(kee-koh-mbeh)

Sieve – Ungo
(oo-ngoh)

Pot – **Sufuria**
(soo-foo-ree-ah)

Kettle – **Birika**
(bee-ree-kah)

Soap – Sabuni
(sah-boo-nee)

Sponge – Sponji
(spoh-njee)

EVERYDAY WORDS, QUESTIONS AND PHRASES

Misemo ya kila siku, maswali na misemo *(mee-seh-moh-yah-yah-kee-lah-see-koo-,-mah-swah-lee-nah-mee-see-moh)*

Welcome – Karibu
(kah-ree-boo)

What is your name? – Jina lako ni nani?
(jee-nah-lah-koh-nee-nah-nee-?)

My name is...(John) – Jina langu ni (John)
(jee-nah-lah-ngoo-nee-John)

How are you? – Unajisikiaje?
(oo-jee-see-kee-ah-jeh-?)

I am well – Niko vizuri
(nee-koh-vee-zoo-ree)

Nothing is new – Hamna jipya
(hah-m-nah-jee-p-yah)

I am fine – Ni mzima
(nee-m-zee-mah)

Fine, thanks. And you? – Salama, asante. Na wewe?
(sah-lah-mah-,-ah-sah-n-teh-,-nah-weh-weh-?)

How old are you? - Je, una umri gani?
(jeh-,-oo-nah-oo-m-ree-gah-nee-?)

How old is he/she? – Je, ana umri gani mvulana/msichana?
(jeh-,-ah-nah-oo-m-ree-gah-nee-m-voo-lah-nah/m-see-chah-nah-?)

I am 20 years old – Nina umri wa miaka 20
(nee-nah-oo-m-ree-wah-mee-ah-kah-ee-shee-ree-nee)

He is ten years old – Mvulana ana umri wa miaka kumi
(m-voo-lah-nah-ah-nah-oo-m-ree-wah-mee-ah-kah-koo-mee)

Where are you from? - Unatoka wapi?
(oo-nah-toh-kah-wah-pee-?)

I am from UK – Ninatoka Uingereza
(nee-nah-toh-kah-oo-ee-ngeh-reh-zah)

Where do you live? – unaishi wapi?
(oo-nah-ee-shee-wah-pee-?)

I live in UK – Ninaishi ndani ya Uingereza
(nee-nah-ee-shee-ndah-nee-yah-oo-ee-ngeh-reh-zah)

Do you speak Swahili? – Je, unazungumza
Kiswahili?
(jeh-,-oo-nah-zoo-ngoo-m-zah-kee-swah-hee-lee-?)

I do speak Swahili – Ninazungumza Kiswahili
(nee-nah-zoo-ngoo-m-zah-kee-swah-hee-lee)

I do not speak Swahili – Sizungumzi kiswahili
(see-zoo-ngoo-m-zee- kee-swah-hee-lee)

Do you come here often? – Je, unakuja hapa
mara nyingi?
(jee, oo-nah-koo-jah-hah-pah-mah-rah-nyee-ngee-?)

I do come here often – Ninakuja hapa mara
nyingi
(nee-nah-koo-jah-hah-pah-mah-rah-nyee-ngee)

I do not come here often – Siji hapa mara nyingi
(see-jee-hah-pah-mah-rah-nyee-ngee)

I am here on vacation – Nipo hapa kwa mapumziko
(nee-poh-hah-pah-kwah-mah-poo-m-zee-koh)

I am in a hurry – Nina haraka
(nee-nah-hah-rah-kah)

Never mind - Usijali
(oo-see-jah-ree)

Where are you going – Je, unakwenda wapi?
(jeh-,-oo-nah-kweh-ndah-wah-pee-?)

I am going to visit… - Ninakwenda ku(m)tembelea
(nee-nah-kweh-ndah-koo-(m-)teh-mbeh-leh-ah)

I will come this morning – Nitakuja asubuhi hii
(nee-tah-koo-jah-ah-soo-boo-hee-hee-ee)

I will come this afternoon/evening – Nitakuja mchana/jioni
(nee-tah-koo-jah m-chah-nah/jee-oh-nee)

I am a student – Mimi ni mwanafunzi
(mee-mee-nee-mwah-nah-foo-nzee)

I am learning Yoruba – Ninajifunza Kiyeruba
(nee-nah-jee-foo-nzah-kee-yeh-roo-bah)

I work – Nafanya kazi
(nah-fah-nyah-kah-zee)

I do not work – Sifanyi kazi
(see-fah-nyee-kah-zee)

I am married – Nimeolewa/nimeoa
(nee-meh-oh-leh-wah/neh-meh-oh-wah)

This is my wife – **Huyu ni mke wagu**
(hoo-yoo-nee-m-keh-wah-ngoo)

Is this your husband? – Huyu ni mume wako?
(hoo-yoo-nee-moo-meh-wah-koh-?)

I am not married – Sijaolewa
(see-jah-oh-leh-wah)

Come here – Njoo hapa
(njoh-oh-hah-pah)

I am hungry – Nina njaa
(nee-nah-njah-ah)

Today I will cook – Leo nitapika
(leh-oh-nee-tah-pee-kah)

I am thirsty for water – Nina kiu ya maji
(nee-nah-kee-oo-yah-mah-jee)

Give me water – Nipe maji
(nee-peh-mah-jee)

I am tired - Nimechoka
(nee-meh-choh-kah)

I am going to sleep – Ninakwenda kulala
(nee-nah-kweh-ndah-koo-lah-lah)

Please – Tafadhali
(tah-fah-dhah-lee)

Thank you – Asante
(ah-sah-n-teh)

You are welcome – Unakaribishwa
(oo-nah-kah-ree-bee-sh-wah)

Sorry – Samahani
(sah-mah-hah-nee)

I understand - Nimeelewa
(nee-meh-eh-leh-wah)

I do not understand – Sijaelewa
(see-jah-eh-leh-wah)

61

I know - Ninajua
(nee-nah-joo-wah)

I do not know – Sijui
(see-joo-wee)

Why – kwanini
(kwah-nee-nee)

What - Nini
(nee-nee)

Who – Nani
(nah-nee)

Where? – Wapi?
(wah-pee-?)

Where is it? – Ipo wapi?
(ee-poh-wah-pee)

Stop – Simama
(see-mah-mah)

Come – Njoo
(njoh-oh)

Come here – Njoo hapa
(njoh-oh-hah-pah)

Go – Ondoka
(oh-ndoh-kah)

How – Vipi
(vee-pee)

How much? – Kiasi gani
(kee-ah-see-gah-nee)

How many? – Ngapi
(ngah-pee)

How far? – Mbali kiasi gani?
(mbah-lee-kee-ah-see-gah-nee-?)

How long? – Muda gani?
(moo-dah-gah-nee-?)

When? – Lini?
(lee-nee-?)

Who is that? – Nani yule?
(nah-nee-yoo-leh-?)

What is this/is? – Hii ni nini?
(hee-eh-nee-nee-nee-?)

What is this for? - Hii ni ya nini?
(hee-ee-nee-yah-nee-nee-?)

What is it called? – Hii inaitwaje?
(hee-ee-ee-nah-ee-twah-jeh-?)

This is – Hii ni
(hee-ee-nee)

What is the matter? – Tatizo ni nini?
(tah-tee-zoh-nee-nee-nee-?)

Nothing – Hamna kitu
(hah-m-nah-kee-too)

What do they call this? – Wanaitaje hii?
(wah-nah-ee-tah-jeh-hee-ee-?)

Can you show me...? – Unaweza kunionyesha?
(oo-nah-weh-zah-koo-nee-oh-nyeh-shah-?)

It is over there – Ipo pale
(ee-poh-pah-leh)

What time is it? – Ni muda gani?
(nee-moo-dah-gah-nee-?)

It is five o'clock – Ni saa kumi na moja kamili
(nee-sah-ah-koo-mee-nah-moh-jah-kah-mee-lee)

I am lost - Nimepotea
(nee-meh-poh-teh-ah)

I have lost my way – Nimepotea njia
(nee-meh-poh-teh-ah-njee-ah)

I have lost my bag – Nimepoteza begi langu
(nee-meh-poh-teh-zah-beh-gee-lah-ngoo)

I have forgotten my way – Nimesahau njia
yangu
(nee-meh-sah-hah-oo-njee-ah-yah-ngoo)

Please help me – Tafadhali nisaidie
(tah-fah-dhah-lee-nee-sah-ee-dee-eh)

I am sick - Ninaumwa
(nee-nah-oo-mwah)

I do not feel well – Sijisikii vizuri
(see-jee-see-kee-ee-vee-zoo-ree)

Get a doctor – Tafuta daktari
(tah-foo-tah-dah-k-tah-ree)

Call the police – Ita polisi
(ee-tah-poh-lee-see)

Be careful – Kuwa makini
(koo-wah-mah-kee-nee)

Fire - Moto
(moh-toh)

Be quick – Wahi
(wah-hee)

Best wishes – Kila la heri
(kee-lah-lah-heh-ree)

Good luck – Uwe na bahati
(oo-weh-nah-bah-hah-tee)

Congratulations – Hongera
(hoh-ngeh-rah)

Praises – Sifa
(see-fah)

Have a good trip – Uwe na safari njema
(oo-weh-nah-sah-fah-ree-njeh-mah)

Merry Christmas – Heri ya Krismasi
(heh-ree-yah-kree-s-mah-see)

Happy birthday – Heri ya siku ya kuzaliwa
(heh-ree-yah-see-koo-yah-koo-zah-lee-wah)

Happy New Year – Heri ya Mwaka Mpya
(heh-ree-yah-mwah-kah-m-pyah)

Happy Easter – Heri ya Pasaka
(heh-ree-yah-pah-sah-kah)

Give my regards to John – Mpe salamu zangu John
(m-peh-sah-lah-moo-zah-ngoo-joh-h-nee)

We are at the hotel – Tupo hotelini
(too-poh-hoh-teh-lee-nee)

Do you have any rooms available? – Je, una vyumba vilivyo wazi? (jeh-,-oo-nah-vyoo-mbah-vee-lee-vyoh-wah-zee-?)

May I see the room? – Naweza kukiona chumba?
(nah-weh-zah-koo-kee-oh-nah-choo-mbah-?)

I do not like it - Sijakipenda
(see-jah-kee-peh-ndah)

This is too small – Hiki ni kidogo sana
(hee-kee-nee-kee-doh-goh-sah-nah)

I would like a room – Ningependa kupata chumba
(nee-ngeh-peh-ndah-koo-pah-tah-choo-mbah)

With a double bed – Kikiwa na vitanda viwili
(kee-kee-wah-nah-vee-tah-ndah-vee-wee-lee)

With twin beds – Kikiwa na vitanda viwili
(kee-kee-wah-nah-vee-tah-ndah-vee-wee-lee)

With a bathroom – Kikiwa na bafu
(kee-kee-wah-nah-bah-foo)

At the front – Mbele
(mbeh-leh)

At the back - Nyuma
(nyoo-mah)

We will be staying – Tutakaa
(too-tah-kah-ah)

Overnight – Kwa usiku
(kwah-oo-see-koo)

Two days – Siku mbili
(see-koo-mbee-lee)

A week - Wiki
(wee-kee)

A fortnight – Wiki mbili
(wee-kee-mbee-lee)

It is too cold – Kuna baridi sana
(koo-nah-bah-ree-dee-sah-nah)

It is too dark – Kuna giza sana
(koo-nah-gee-zah-sah-nah)

Give me a large room – Nipe chumba kikubwa
(nee-peh-choo-mbah-kee-koo-bwah)

What is the price? – Bei gani?
(beh-ee-gah-nee-?)

I will take it - Nitachukua
(nee-tah-choo-koo-ah)

My key, please – Funguo yangu, tafadhali
(foo-ngoo-oh-yah-ngoo-,-tah-fah-dhah-lee)

Waiter – Mhudumu (mvulana)
(m-hoo-doo-moo) ((m-voo-lah-nah)

Waitress – Mhudumu (msichana)
(m-hoo-doo-moo(m-see-chah-nah)

Can I have the menu please – Naweza kupata menyu tafadhali
(nah-weh-zah-koo-pah-tah-meh-nyoo-tah-fah-dhah-lee)

Meal - Chakula
(chah-koo-lah)

Breakfast – Chakula cha asubuhi
(chah-koo-lah-chah-ah-soo-boo-hee)

Lunch – Chakula cha mchana
(chah-koo-lah-chah-m-chah-nah)

Dinner – Chakula cha usiku
(*chah-koo-lah-chah-oo-see-koo*)

What would you like? – Ungependa nini?
(*oo-ngeh-peh-ndah-nee-nee-?*)

May I have...? – Naweza kupata......?
(*nah-weh-zah-koo-pah-tah-......-?*)

Have you had enough? – Umekinai
(*oo-meh-kee-nah-ee*)

Are you full? – Umeshiba
(*oo-meh-shee-bah*)

I have had enough – Nimekinai
(*nee-meh-kee-nah-ee*)

I am full – Nimeshiba
(*nee-meh-shee-bah*)

That is enough right – Hiyo imetosha si ndio
(*hee-yoh-ee-nah-toh-shah-see-ndee-oh*)

It is bad – Ni mbaya
(*mbah-yah*)

It is good – Ni nzuri
(*nee-nzoo-ree*)

ABOUT MOTHERLAND LITERATURE

Motherland Literature is made up of a group of professional African translators who are passionate about teaching and preserving African languages and culture.

With over 20 years of professional translating experience between us, you can rest assured that all Motherland Literature books are accurate, concise and informative.

All our books are proudly written by a respective native of the language that is being covered.

This ensure's that we deliver an authentic body of work, with nothing being added or taken away from the historicity of the language.

We take great pride in our books and aim to assist you in learning the African language of your choice. Whether Amharic or Zulu, we're here to help.

If you found this book to be useful and informative, please consider leaving us a review on Amazon.

Thank you,

MOTHERLAND LITERATURE

Printed in Great Britain
by Amazon

83121763R00047